The Uni
Verse

...a journey into our amazing cosmos

by

Tom Mach

Hill Song Press

Lawrence, Kansas

The Uni Verse

Published by:

Hill Song Press
P. O. Box 486
Lawrence, KS 66044
www.HillSongPress.com

Library of Congress Control No. 2007924020
ISBN# 978-0-9745159-8-4

Printed in the USA by Edwards Brothers Inc.

Foreword

Readers who are familiar with my historical novels, such as *Sissy!* and *All Parts Together* may be surprised to learn that I have also authored a book of poetry. I have always enjoyed writing poetry, and have had some of my poems published.

But while I did not intend to publish a book of poetry at this time, I became mesmerized by the sheer beauty and wonder of Walt Whitman's *Leaves of Grass*. I had studied Whitman and his poetry as part of my research for *All Parts Together.* One evening a thought struck me. What if Mr. Whitman were alive today and possessed all the knowledge of the 21st century? What kind of poetry would he write? In that vein, I tried to sense the same things that perhaps Mr. Whitman might have sensed.

The universe is an immense canvas, and the prospect of writing about it was rather challenging. I began writing *The Uni Verse* in a spirit of both humility and exploration. I realized that the universe is so vast that there was an excellent chance that there is another world out there very similar to ours. Given that, what are the chances that God has souls other than those on Earth that He cares about? Anyway, that poses an interesting thought, and I suggested that possibility in *The Uni Verse.*

I saw the movie "Astronaut Farmer" about a man who builds his own spacecraft and blasts off into orbit—successfully. Maybe it's a secret dream some of us have, a dream about exploring new worlds. Perhaps the poems in this book will help catapult you into this dream and allow you to experience the incredible thrill of "being out there."

Have a great journey in *The Uni Verse*!

The Uni Verse **by Tom Mach**

Part 1: Song of Beginnings

I.

We celebrate ourselves, and sing ourselves,
and what we assume, the universe will assume.
For every atom belonging to you as good belongs to all.
Loaf now and invite your soul.
Peer through this astronomer's lens, and observe a
heavenly body suspended on…nothing.
But I cannot focus since earthly matters cloud over me,
and computer surfers surround me,
and daily problems encompass me,
Thus, I depart now as air and whisk into the twilight,
into the darkness of what we know as space,
into the adventure we call our final frontier.

Once I leave, you will hardly know who I am or what I mean.
But I shall bring wisdom to you nevertheless.
If you fail to find me, still be encouraged;
Missing me at one star, search another.
I stop somewhere, waiting for you.

II

As I lay prone, my head dizzying
and the sinews of my being stretched,
I caught a vision greater than the width of my soul.
Lemaître, a Belgian voice, went on about a primeval atom
which started the Universe with an explosion,
pushing galaxies away from each other at speeds
higher than Mach numbers, faster than light.
On the heels of the Belgian priest came another voice,
that of a Shrewsbury naturalist who shook out the
cobwebs of thought of Anaximander, an ancient Greek
who gave the name *apeiron* to the essence of all things.

Limitless and indeterminate, mysterious and unseen,
but somehow a connection between life and non-life,
apeiron answered nothing and the darkness grasped it not.
For the explorer of the primeval atom from which it all began
finds not the source of knowledge and still thirsts.

III

O Inventor of Computers, O Philosophers of Wisdom,
O Ye Scientists of Fact, O Ye Darwinian Dogmatists,
I cannot fathom the depth of it all, so how can you?
I cannot see this primeval atom hurling through space,
only to detonate into a cataclysmic outburst,
emanating round balls of matter and blinding helium stars.
Is my mind so feeble that only the Wise Men of science
can grasp it, and not the Wise Men of religion?
I cannot grasp eternity, let alone this primeval atom,
from whence no one knows the mystery of its *own* birth,
let alone the birth you claim it gave to this universe.

The elephant, the horse, the cow, the bird, the insect...
So fortunate are they that do not question like us,
wanting answers to life questions, as to cause and effect,
but simply being content with existence and accepting
it as if there be no need to question or test or explore.

IV

Great are myths, but I do not delight in them.
Great is life, both real and mystical.
Great is love, both imagined and sincere.
Great are the stars as they dot the sky.
Great are the planets that watch our folly.
Great are the comets, which visit with regularity.
Great are the meteorites, though I fear them deeply.
Great is time, with no ending or beginning.
Great is space, though I cannot grasp its emptiness.
Great is the universe, which I do not understand.
Greater still, the answer as to why we are here.

Children go outdoors to play,
and they study the webs of spiders
and the changing faces of clouds
and ask questions that confound adults,
and a few will become adults who explore new worlds.

V

Fog covers my eyes, yet I perceive saviors in white
chattering something about forceps and a "yes, doctor"
from one of the nurse angels bathed in fluorescent.
Only for a moment am I conscious of my body, but
as I lapse back into the deepest space, I hear a voice.
Hesiod, an ancient Greek poet, revered so by Homer,
calls me, bids me to join him as he shepherds his lambs
while the Heliconian Muses sing a song of the Cosmos.
Zeus thunders in; his queen Hera, tiptoes through the naked skies,
past Poseidon, who holds and shakes the earth
against a dark Night pierced by bright Selene.
I had hoped it might be the ancients who have the solution.

But my questions chase elusive answers.
Ancient Greeks describe the universe as a stage,
while the Norse make it an enormous tree circling the earth,
implanted in the world of the Dead and their gods.
So, like Odysseus, are you not swept ashore, exhausted?

VI.

Immersed in the quagmire of mythology am I?
Well, free that chariot and take me to the Starship Enterprise,
where Captain Kirk will beam me to the apron of the cosmos.
Transport me to the primitive past, unclose the curtain
that separates irresolute time from unfathomable space.
I want not the fictional, dreamy world of Roddenberry.
Whisk me past floating debris we call asteroids,
past those flaming torches we've named comets.
My true destiny is to reach for the outer hem where stars,
those hydrogen-producing nuclear furnaces
light up just a mere fraction of the blackness of space.

What's that? Stars are created and then die?..like us?
An inter-stellar cloud becomes their embryo
and helium and hydrogen their sperm.
The human mother screams her contractions
while the violence of the cloud thunders its anger.

VII.

These wise men all talk at once—
Aristotle, Copernicus, Kepler, Newton, and Einstein.
Like fine sculptors they chip away at the truth,
coming from different directions,
using different chisels,
but raising more questions than before,
they end up with crushed stone
rather than a finished statue of understanding.
Aristotle questioned what caused everything,
Copernicus said we were not the center of everything
and mathematicians claimed to predict everything.

Maybe our universe
is too large a canvas for us to study.
Maybe we need to examine, like Whitman,
that child's simple question: "What is grass?"
before we can advance to the next grade.

VIII.

Men of Science tell us that attraction created the stars,
that particles in these clouds have mutual desires
and that gravitational force prompts them to accelerate,
much like, I suppose, men accelerate to their first love.
But as the professor writes his formulae on the board,
explaining how atoms collide with such violence
that they strip off their electrons, becoming atomic nuclei,
which, in turn, repel other nuclei, while these forsaken electrons
repel other electrons, such that the cloud erupts in heat,
I cannot help but imagine that perhaps violence is not
something authored by man but given us by the stars.

I journey onward now toward these glowing clouds.
A proto-star, which for all its heat and light
is yet but a cloud of gas that can either become a star
if it is massive enough or else can be demoted
and doomed forever as a lowly planet.

IX.

A child once asked me what is space and laughed
as I cried in the snot of my ignorance.
I thought I knew what it was, distances, measurements,
and what was in-between was space.
Is that not true? Is not space sold like a commodity?
Indeed--You can buy space in a newspaper,
space in a parking lot, space on a airplane.
We all sell it, but do we know what it is?
I most assuredly do not, especially now
as I fly though the darkness of nothingness
at bewildering speeds, in a hurry to go nowhere.

Is there no end to this tormenting universe,
as I go on at speeds I cannot comprehend?
Or perhaps I am able to traverse the all of everything.
Are there not multiple universes, perhaps infinitely so
and have I hardly even begun my quest?

X.

My head spins at a confusing pace
when I think about multiple universes,
since my pitiful mind cannot conceive of that.
No, better that I look at just one universe!
Still, even then I have to consider multiple galaxies.
Thus, I insist you escort me to the Milky Way,
the mother of our solar system, which scientists say
is home to 400 billion stars, planets, and nebulae.
Are you trying to impress me that the Milky Way
has a diameter of one hundred thousand light years?

How did you measure that?
What measuring tool did you use?
And how many lifetimes would you burn up
in assessing its length from tip to tip?
Or...why assess it at all?

XI.

"Wake up," a nightingale voice blossoms in my ear.
I open my eyes to a vague awareness of a nurse,
mumble my displeasure at her rude interruption
and drift back into the blackness of space
as I tumble along to a comical, teasing song:
Do You Know The Way to Milky Way?
But the line does not require an answer from me,
for I've already arrived there, feeling inadequate
among the 400 billion bodies of matter,
such that I am mere protoplasm
in an enormous ocean of life.

Yes, I am ***in*** Mesier's catalog, and not just looking at it,
and I see hydrogen clouds blinking with lights,
and I know that out there among all those clusters,
among all those nebulae, is Earth,
an insignificant dust of matter.

XII.

Greek sages say the goddess Hera breastfed Heracles.
But as the baby sucked, she learned it was not hers
and tore her breast from his hungry mouth, and
droplets of milk spread across the heavens and
the galaxy was henceforth christened Milky Way.
But Ovid claims it as the highway of the gods,
and its tortuous path leads to Jupiter's palace.
To me, however, it is a mesmerizing haiku:
Milky Way flowing gently
down dark path
to capture light from afar.

A forever-pregnant woman is the Milky Way,
with spiral arms of stars, nebulae, and matter,
and her breasts bulge with constellations.
and her womb contains globular star clusters.
But no child therein, for She is very old indeed.

XIII.

Nothing ever rests in this busy universe.
All matter is constantly in motion.
Helium fires induce the stars to sparkle,
and comets zing like flaming arrows,
but they return after a long absence
to repeat their endless flight.
Asteroids fly through the blackness of space,
and make senseless, eon-long orbits.
So, too, do galaxies continue on their move,
while the planets within circle about
the nearest star in carousel fashion.

Does Death not even *exist* in space?
Do objects move because there is nothing
to slow them from the Big Bang?
No friction, no blocks to retard their journey?
or...*was* there even a Big Bang?

XIV.

This constant movement...be it akin to music?
Indeed, composer Gustav Holst believed so
with tone poems in his Opus thirty-two.
Poet Weldon wrote that the Poem of the Universe
possessed neither rhythm nor rhyme because "some God
recites the wondrous song a stanza at a time."
Music, rhythm, flowing, ebbing, moving.
If I listen hard, I hear not a sound,
so the music cometh from my soul
and not from the stirring of the Milky Way.
Yea, from a stirring in my heart.

If I were to set this galaxy into song
I would not have enough percussion instruments,
nor would I have sufficient trumpets
to mimic the intensity of it movements,
nor violins to soften its grace.

XV.

"He's rapidly losing his pulse, doctor!"
Panic is evident in the nurse's voice while
A male blurts out "Code Blue" and I can sense
my body being wheeled somewhere while
more shrill voices rise to a crescendo and I wonder
why this alarm when I am a peace with the universe.
Ah, the Universe! I soar through the Milky Way,
as I approach what may be my solar system.
But is it? I wonder as I see two stars in the center
of swirling ellipses of planetary bodies,
and I approach a blue-white earthlike globe.

Perhaps this is what space sailors experienced—
Stafford, Irwin, Armstrong, pioneers all,
as they entered the earth's atmosphere
and watched in wonder at its huge arc
and observed how night and day kissed.

XVI.

Somehow, I come to dry land without touching the sea,
but I thrill at being able to feel something solid,
rather than the helpless void of a space swim.
I hear foreign screams, vengeful sounds and I hide,
in fear that my life may be in danger.
Instead, I see a bleeding creature struggling,
a beam on his shoulders, forced to march
as a band of angry, vile creatures curse at him,
and I wonder what this being could have done
to reap such vengeance and hate and
how this fit in with the peace of the universe.

After nailing him to a pole,
they raise him up and taunt him,
while others wail in deep hurt,
and my heart, too, bleeds for this stranger
as I wondered what he had done.

XVII.

Night came quickly with a pale green sky and no moon,
and a chill touches me, naked in my loneliness.
Perhaps I've crossed a time dimension,
and I am back on Earth in an earlier age.
But no, the heavens sparkle with unfamiliar stars.
Am I a witness to what no earthling has ever seen,
and should I be the envy of every astronaut?
But I have no hunger for devouring it all.
Come from long distance, have I.
Lonely man.
Hunger for touch, for someone.

Two sunrises burst through the morning
and I awake, trembling.
Gone is that creature on the pole.
Gone too are those hateful beings.
Gone must I be, lest I die as well.

XVIII.

Somehow I feel caught between two worlds,
one where I look down and see white angels,
their gloved fingers bloody as they explore my innards;
the other, a world that is boundless and beautiful
and mysterious and frightful.
Yet I choose the latter because I have not found
the essence of all things and need to know
if it can even ***be*** discovered.
So I travel again through the blackness of it all,
straining for any sign of home where
white angels with bloody gloves do not reside.

Instead, I find a rocky, metallic ball
rolling toward me, irresolute, challenging.
My heart beating wildly,
I dodge its righteous path,
and it moves on, just as I move on.

XIX.

I think we have the wrong idea about space.
It is not a cold, dark void at all,
but a collection of colonies,
each with its own charmed and loving beings,
and each with its own culture and values,
and each coexisting with its orbital neighbors.
Maybe it is Earth that has this problem
of ownership and entitlement,
of fear and suspicion,
of intolerance and greed,
while stopping love with legislated walls..

We earthlings get caught up in ourselves,
convinced this marble on which we live
is a immense beach ball dominating the pool,
and that if we could, we'd make other worlds
subject to our sadly distorted whims.

XX.

I imagine myself as Charlie Brown in a Peanuts cartoon
telling Lucy that I think there must be a tiny star out there,
a tiny star that is ***my*** star,
explaining to her how alone I am here on earth
among millions of people,
while that tiny star is out there, also alone,
among millions and millions of stars.
"Does that make any sense, Lucy?" I ask.
"Certainly," she answers, shaking her head,
"It means you're cracking up, Charlie Brown."
And maybe that truly is my problem.

After all, as these wonders unroll,
no one else wonders
but me.
So maybe this is a movie
only God can understand.

XXI.

God. Yahweh. Almighty....
All short names for such an enormous Wonderment.
Did He actually set about creating everything
from only His thought?
Are we to believe that in the beginning was the Word
and the Word was with God
and the Word ***was*** God,
so that the Word came down to earth
to be crucified by evil men,
nailed to a pole, just like
that creature I saw?

My mind ponders the imponderable—
Could He have been the Christ
come again to be mocked and sacrificed
as an innocent Lamb
for the sins of yet ***another*** world?

XXII.

I do not recognize the black robed man at first
until he gives me a crucifix to kiss
and sprinkles me with holy water.
My mouth does not say the words bursting in my head
--I don't need the last rites, Father.
But he does not hear me
--Cleanse me of sin with hyssop, Lord,
  that I may be purified.
I cannot shut out his monotonic words:
-- *Our help is in the Name of the Lord*
  Who made Heaven and Earth

The Lord must have made the universe
because *apeiron* answers nothing.
But if the darkness grasped it not,
how in my feeble mind
do I grasp God?

The Uni Verse **by Tom Mach**

Part 2: Song of the Solar System

I.

Earth, sun, moon, and planets—the only Universe I know,
like a child in a playpen confined by his walls.
Twinkling stars then were only night-lights,
and I knew not of helium furnaces.
Enter Kodak and pictures from space.
So now we live on a bluish-white orb,
no longer looking at a man in the moon,
but at a pock-marked ball of yellow.
Thank you for naming its craters, ye scientists,
thank you for Tsiolkovsy, Schrodinger, and Aristarchus,
but I prefer the vision of a moonstruck poet.

Shakespeare blamed the moon for Caesar's defeat,
but my haiku praises its splendor:
Moon begotten, moon of old,
Earth hides you.
Your beauty unfolds in time.

II.

Astrology and astronomy, twin sciences
until the two parted ways forever.
After Galileo opened the universe with a telescope,
the mathematician caressed astronomy,
concerned over distances and dimensions,
while the philosopher embraced astrology,
pondering the meaning of heavenly bodies.
In ages past, astrologers danced with astronomers
like children caught up in a carnival,
soaking in the newness of it all,
and awed by its deep mystery.

Now astronomers have erased the allure
of those wise, camel-riding astrologers
who once trailed a God-directed star.
But could Reverend Hopkins have set
"O ***Planetary Alignment*** of Wonder" to music?

III.

O ye astrologers of old,
O ye guides for Chaldean kings
O ye sages for Roman emperors
O ye consultants for Arabian princes
O ye influencers of Renaissance artists...
on what basis can ye say the planets
determine our destinies?
Thou hath stroked the heavenly canvas
with a righteous rod
with which ye direct the sun, moon, stars, and planets
to alone foretell our fate.

Sun rising in Scorpio?
Moon descending in Pisces?
Ah! Saturn returns, but observe
the Mars effect,
but not thy free will.

IV.

Enter astrologer,
and tell me again why I am stubborn
if my sun sign is Taurus
but vacillate if I'm in Gemini?
Does Venus rule me,
or does Mercury?
How do distant constellations
affect, effect, and infect my life?
Once only emperors were consulted
on the fate of their nation and themselves
Now, a commoner's money gets a reading.

No room for God or reasoning.
No room for explanation.
Find a horoscope,
Find your sign,
Define your life.

V.

Whitman called it a "splendid silent sun,
with all his beams full-dazzling,"
but I call it an unquenchable star,
of whom a thousand songs were sung.
God carved the night into day
with this star.
Planets merrily orbit about
this luminous centerpiece,
giving it profound homage
with their constant motion—
like wooden horses circling about
a demanding motor.

The sun also turns
about its massive belly,
flaring out its heat,
as spots mark its burning face,
its five billion year face.

VI.

O bright sun
O glowing Mother of all nuclear reactors,
I do not know whether to curse or bless you.
You give us dazzling sunsets and hopeful stories.
You brighten us when clouds disappear.
Yet poets like John Donne condemn you,
dubbing you a "busy old fool,"
whose rays shine on both the wicked and the good.
I know flowers need you for their sparkle,
and plants raise their leafy arms to praise you,
you even make a distraught child smile.

But why do you interfere so in battle?
You arose early on a Normandy beachhead,
illuminating enemy positions,
and when you hid your face and blackened the sky,
the Lydians and the Medes ceased their battle.

VII.

I wish for pre-Galilean times
when the Earth was the centerpiece
and humankind, the center
But the man from Pisa swung his scope
toward the sky and crushed the tenet
of our importance to God's handiwork
so that the sun did not revolve about us,
but we about the sun.
Now only the moon circles us.
And the sun does not rise to greet us,
but we rise to greet the sun.

Copernicus too,
with his heliocentric ideas,
confirmed a celestial rhythm and path
and made God a mathematician
the way He made it all.

VIII.

Now all is rhythm and rhyme
Planets knew their place and stage
No chaos in creation but in ***us.***
Always and ever, from age to age.

Eight new bodies
in Century Seventeen.
and dozens more
as more became seen.

Tell me where is fancy bred,
in the heart or in the head?
Yes, dreams cannot be measured,
but a planet's motions can be read.

> *Planets start their long trek, then*
> *boomerang*
> *to renew their tiresome course.*

IX.

Pluto, seen in nineteen-thirty,
deep in the realms of space.
Farthest child from Mother Sun,
you finally showed your face.

Yet seventy-six years later
Astronomers deny your fame,
demoting you to mere dwarf,
no longer a planet by name.

But to me you still are my planet
and Charon is still your dear moon.
You face each other in your travel through space,
both spinning, yet both in tune.

I dare not embark upon your soil.
I would surely find it barren.
Only dust and ash and rocky ground
No bloom, no Rose of Sharon.

Lonely object far away
we caught you.
Now you reveal your secrets.

X.

Why dost thou lie on thy side,
Uranus, as thou art so strangely named?
Did a planet careen thee out of place
as is most commonly claimed?

Voyager counted thy many rings
all told, there are nine we saw
Thou art an eerie color of green
Thy wonders wrap us with awe.

Laden with twenty-two moons
as thou dost orbit the sun.
Lethargic and yet steadfast,
Eighty-four years to our one.

Greek god of all sky no more,
tilt and spin,
dark halos surround thy crown.

XI.

Neptune, your gale winds
whisk me off your globe.
Clouds shadow your barren land.
You wear a gaseous robe.

Your mysterious dark spot
would swallow our Earth.
And four rings, narrow and faint
cover your gigantic girth.

Trailing clouds streak
and methane does color you blue,
while your noticeable dark spots
complete the inexplicable you.

Once a mad god of earthquakes
and sea god,
now only a gas giant.

XII.

Sailing over its surface
with eighteen moons in sight.
Prepare for an orbit of ten hours.
Prepare for a very short night.

When we conjure up Saturn
we invoke its many rings,
as they circle this great planet
and make us question things.

Are they ice or snowballs?
From whence did these rings come?
Yet it does not matter what they are;
their beauty makes us numb.

Ye god of agriculture,
sow peace seeds.
We love your marvelous rings.

XIII.

O Jupiter, king of planets,
O dinosaur globe sublime
A thousand Earths contain you.
O planet of ancient time.

Mozart wrote your symphony,
and Galileo your moons did see
Asians call you the Wood Star
to honor your majesty.

Your gravity catches comets
that crash into your sphere.
Your Great Red Spot truly is
an Earth-sized storm to fear.

Supreme god of Roman lore
once stood tall,
symbol of justice no more.

IX.

How many trips to Mars
did science fiction writers write?
When Viking Landers found no life,
believers gave up their fight.

Lines on your surface,
canals they were not,
color changes meant naught,
so what have we got?

We have a Red Planet
that may have had rivers.
Since ***life*** may have been there,
it gives us the shivers.

O red son of Jupiter,
god of war,
we sob with your battle cry.

X.

Thou hast neither moon nor rings,
still thou are a true delight.
Thou art a jewel of the sky,
a round ball of radiant light.

Venus, we call you a sister,
born the same time as Earth,
from the same nebula,
and similar mass and girth.

Yet carbon dioxide fills your sky;
oceans have you not,
and your runaway greenhouse
makes you extremely hot.

Elegant statue of you,
Love Goddess.
Mother of Roman people.

XI.

No atmosphere to scatter light;
Mercury, your sky be always dark.
Your craters be both deep and wide,
your landscape always stark.

Smaller than a Saturn moon,
with fastest spin about the sun,
Until Mariner examined you close,
your surface was known by none.

Helium blankets your curved cliffs,
and solar tides still sway,
while your dust-covered hills
watch an earthrise every day.

O god of profit and trade,
Mercury,
winged one, swift planet thou art.

The Uni Verse **by Tom Mach**

Part 3: Song of the Earth

A Sonnet to Our Earth

To Earth we sing a sonnet
for many different reasons.
We love your lofty bonnet
along with your four seasons.
Wash us with your rain,
A breeze for us caress.
Give us food and grain.
and beauty you possess.
Problem is we take for granted
all the wonders God has given.
A beauteous forest so enchanted,
Gone are sins that He's forgiven.

Now we cry out as one voice
for Your wonders, we rejoice.

The Eternal Struggle

Earth's gravity is a stubborn old fool,
forcing us to stay grounded
even if we do *not* misbehave.

Newton and his cursed apple
caused mass and acceleration formulae
to explode on Harvard chalkboards.

Suicide candidates and politicians alike
must land hard to a demanding earth,
while windless kites will always crash,
because Gravity ignores young sobs
and hates defiant birds and planes.

Heavenly orbs spin in wide paths,
taunting Gravity to suck them in,
and the fight goes on for eons,
One force pulling,
Another force pushing,
while the inhabitants of earth
are blind not only to the struggle above
but to the struggle within.

Unseen atoms move, eternally restless
as electrons race about nuclei,
taunting opposing forces, daring
others to join them to form molecules.

Professorial eyeballs
through electronic microscopes
observe the ancient dance,
yet they are not entertained
as they compose theories
few understand
or want to.

Yet the struggle continues,
force and anti-force,
on an immense canvas
or on the point of pin.

Yes, restless universe.
          restless earth.
                    restless man.
Ah, motion…
the eternal struggle.

The Moon Am I

I am the Moon.
I have witnessed dinosaurs
roaming your Earth
and I have also seen the comet's
impact that destroyed them.

I am the Moon.
I wept when I saw a great flood cover your Earth,
and I wondered if your planet would be devoid of life.

I am the Moon.
I was worshiped by the pharaohs as a god,
while the ancient Greeks called me a goddess.

I am the Moon.
I saw Galileo examine my craters
through a device called a telescope.

I am the Moon.

I have seen wars circling your globe,
and questioned what you meant by peace.

I am the Moon.

I awoke to the thumping of human footsteps on my soil.
I have heard your utterance about a giant step for
mankind.

I am the Moon.

I miss those days when lovers gazed upon me,
and when they composed songs in my name.

I am the Moon.

I am no longer admired or noticed by you,
and I am lonely.

No More Rivers

The loam gently squeezes
the living juices from the earth's mantle,
crowning it
with rivulets
that add
refreshment and joy
to men
who will father
generations
of sightless souls
who will ask:

"What *is* a river?"

Technology vs. Nature

If I had but one wish
I'd talk to a fish
and ask it how it survived
when technology arrived.

Eons ago, I'd say
you saw a simpler day
No dams to block you,
nor construction crew
to encase you in cement
and so on you went.

enjoying God's gift
with no technology shift.

Designs From Space

I wonder what it's like
to observe Earth from space.
Cape Cod is a gray anchor
while Cape Town is an arm reaching out
across the blue ocean.

I wonder what it's like
to see borderless countries.
Kansas City floodplains
and Kalamazoo gridlines
and open prairie.

I wonder what it's like
to watch an ocean without boats
and snow-covered poles
and pale-yellow clouds
over shrinking jungles.

His Mind

God placed His hand
over His earthly creation
to protect our land
from deadly radiation.

We are third from the sun
but number one
in God's mind.

Oxygen did He give
so we may survive
More that just live,
He helped us to thrive.

We orbit the sun
but we are number one
in God's mind.

The Unseen Crowd

I didn't know the extent of our universe
until I placed a drop of water
on a slide
and stared at civilizations
through a microscope

I didn't know the extent of our universe
until a chemist told me about molecules
made up of atoms
with each atom a solar system
onto itself.

I didn't know the extent of our universe
until I stood on a sandy beach
wondering
how many lifetimes it would take
to count the grains.

Observations

A night crawler hugs the earth
Muddy ground
Sunrise finds it on a hook.

Restless moon pressing ocean.
Stretch waters.
Wash away Suzy's castle.

Ancient cavern, cold, dark, damp.
Stalactite.
Dripping water, more sculpture.

Life Tunnels

A tiny seed
sucked through a straw,
- blending

with the milk of life,
- burning

with the fire of anger,
- bending

with the walls of strife,
- churning

with a vortex of chaos
forever, it seems,
- rising

for hope of true joy,
but swimming instead
into the lips of death.

An Interview with the Earth

If the Earth could speak
what would it say about its formation?
What would it say when collisions
shook its foundation?

Would it heave from the
thumping of large beasts?
Or laugh from the superstitions
of ancient priests?

Did it pride itself with the tombs
of Egyptian pharaohs?
Or feel the sharp pain
of enemy arrows?

Did it clear a path for buffalos
racing through the field?
Did it smile with the farmer
over his abundant yield?

Or suffer with parched lips
through the Dust Bowl?
And did it linger
over a broken soul?

It think it also cried
when highways were built.
We encased the ground
but shared not the guilt.

A Perspective

Babylonians wanted others to see the world,
so they preserved it on a clay tablet.
Greeks studied the moon and planets
and said our world also had to be round.
Medieval scholars thought our world large

But Columbus set sail anyway,.
and weary journeys circling the globe
inspired the Renaissance.

Later, technology stepped in
and Neil Armstrong stepped on the moon
and *voila!*--the world became small
again.

Wishing Upon a Star

When the evening gets dark
I may look up, but will I see
a special star making an arc,
wanting a wish from me?

Should I make a wish for me
if a shooting star at night
blinks and winks at me
as it moves far out of sight?

No, when I wish upon a star
my great desire I won't see.
How can an object out so far
know that here and now I be?

Core Value

Earth, if I drilled deep
what would I reap?
A light, brittle crust,
Twenty-five miles deep.

Then a mantle I'd find.
of molten, silicate rock.
intense heat from behind,
an oven below mankind.

Finally, I'd get down to the core
a mass that rotates from within.
A huge iron magnet to explore
attracting mystery forevermore.

A Satellite Ending

Sputnik I
Sputnik II
Explorer I
Explorer II.

Satellites so high
Satellites that test
Satellites that spy
and all the rest.

Coordinates aligned?
Yes, there's Maple Street
Instead, you chose to find
a nuclear spreadsheet
and Armageddon.

Lord, with all this clutter in the heavens above
help our technology guide us to Your love.

Eternity

Like Whitman, I know I am deathless
and I will live on because my soul lives on,
and the living will search for answers,
while the dead will have already found them.
Nature gives me a clue to eternity.
The grass hides in the winter
but resurrects in the spring.
And those great souls who have lived,
Mozart, Plato, Tolstoy, and Lincoln
cannot just lie barren forever.
They have music to compose
and philosophy to study
and books to write
and slaves to free.
And the greatest Soul who has always lived,
had died so that we can truly ***be*** free,
forever.

A Child's Closing Prayer

The lake is smooth and as still as death,
but an occasional cricket shatters the silence.
"Grandpa," I begin, but he shushes me.
"Let your soul drink it in," he says.
I follow his gaze to the evening sky,
all pierced with white dots
while a round white moon
touches the darkness.
"God is here," he whispers.
"Where?" I ask, frowning.
But I see his smile,
and I understand.

List of Credits for Photos & Illustrations

Page	Item	Source Credit
Front Cover		National Aeronautics and Space Administration (NASA)
1	Fireworks Galaxy	Gemini Observatory/AURA
47	Solar System	NASA
65	The Earth	NASA
70	The Moon	www.astronomy.com
72	River	www.hanifworld.com
77	Fish on a Hook	www.newfunpages.com
77	Sand castle	www.ariedencreations.com
77	Stalactite	No. Illinois University
91	Tom Mach	Virginia Mach
Back Cover		NASA

Meet the Poet

Tom Mach has two grown children, Michelle and Mark, and lives with his wife Virginia in Lawrence, Kansas. Tom is no stranger to poetry, having been published in *The Colors of Life* (The International Library of Poetry), *Parnassus Magazine*, *Eternal Echoes* (Poetry Press), and *Dreams* (Poetry Press), as well as other publications.

Tom is a member in the Kansas Authors Club, the Kansas Writers Association, and the California Writers Club—as well as a Fellow with the Kansas Center For The Book. He has also given talks and held writing workshops.

While doing research for his historical novel, *All Parts Together*, Mach studied the astounding poetry of Walt Whitman. "The poet's *Leaves of Grass*," he says, "spoke volumes on the human condition and on the tenacity of the human spirit." It was Whitman's poetry that inspired this collection of Mach's poems.

A Thank You Letter

Dear God,

To understand an artist,

we need to understand her art.

To understand an architect,

we need to understand his architecture.

To understand the Creator,

we need to understand His creation.

and it is amazing, God,
just as You are amazing.

Thank You…for everything.

Save on your next purchase of *Uni Verse, Sissy!* or *All Parts Together*

$2 off list price for any copy

Clip coupon below and mail with payment.

Enclosed is my check or money order for

___copies of *Uni Verse* @ **$8.95** [reg. $10.95]
___ copies of *Sissy!* at **$13.95** [reg: $15.95]
___copies of *All Parts Together* at **$14.95** [reg: $16.95]

Total of above: $______________
Add: $2.05 for shipping per copy
Add: sales tax if Kansas resident

TOTAL ENCLOSED: ________________________

Hill Song Press P O Box 486 Lawrence, KS 66044

NAME____
ADDRESS______________________________________
CITY_________________STATE_____ZIP___________

www.HillSongPress.com